SMART BRAIN RIGHT BRAIN

Robots and Robotics

Om KIDZ
An imprint of Om Books International

First Published in 2021 by

Om Books International

Corporate & Editorial Office
A-12, Sector 64, Noida 201 301
Uttar Pradesh, India
Phone: +91 120 477 4100
Email: editorial@ombooks.com
Website: www.ombooksinternational.com

Sales Office
107, Ansari Road, Darya Ganj
New Delhi 110 002, India
Phone: +91 11 4000 9000
Email: sales@ombooks.com

Author: Shweta Sinha
Editor: Kirti Pathak
Art & Design: Anshuman Pandey, Gaurav Bhandari, Harish Arya

ISBN: 978-93-5276-840-0

Printed in India

10 9 8 7 6 5 4 3 2 1

CONTENTS

1. What Is a Robot?

Does the word '**Robot**' bring to your mind images such as these?

Robots that look like people with hands, legs and a head are called '**humanoid**' or '**android**'. However, not all robots resemble humans. These are robots too:

Robots can vacuum clean your home or mow your lawn. They can even change your cat's litter box.

POCKET FACT

The first humanoid robot, Elektro, was launched in 1939. It was seven feet tall and spoke about 700 words.

A robot is an automatic machine. It is designed to do one or more tasks faster, safer and better than humans do. It can be programmed to follow specific instructions and to gather information from its environment to do its work.

Famous Robots

Curiosity is the biggest rover ever sent to Mars. It is as big as a car. It has a robot arm to drill and collect samples of rocks and dust. Lasers help it identify the chemicals in the rocks. And it has cameras to click pictures to send back to Earth.

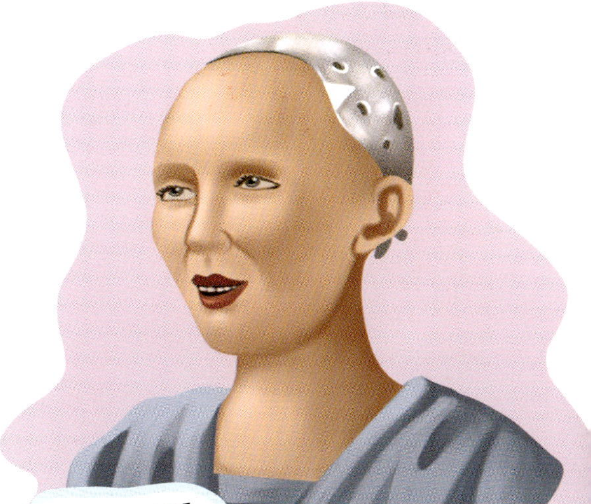

Sofia is a social humanoid robot with an eye-catching presence. She talks like a human and has even given interviews. She is the first robot to be made a citizen of a country.

DID YOU KNOW?

The world's biggest robot is a 51-feet tall walking, fire-breathing dragon.

What is the role of a robot?

Some robots like remote controlled toy-cars are made to entertain. Surgeons use robotics to perform surgeries that need great precision. Robots are extremely useful in exploring space where human travel is not yet possible. Robots are also ideal for dangerous jobs like defusing bombs and exploring the ocean bed.

Who builds the robots?

Robotics engineers are the scientists who design, build and operate robots. They invent new ways to use robots. They decide what to build the robots with, and also program the robots to actually perform their tasks.

POCKET FACT

Robots are commonly used in factories to assemble cars, package goods or stick labels. Some robots even build other robots.

Robot structure

Robots are mostly made of metals and plastics. They have three main parts:

1. **Controller** - The 'brain' of a robot which is run by a computer program. The program has instructions for the robot's moving parts to follow.

2. **Sensors** - Sensors tell the robot about its surroundings. They work like the eyes and ears of a robot.

3. **Mechanical Parts** - The motors, piston, gears and other moving parts that actually perform the robot's tasks.

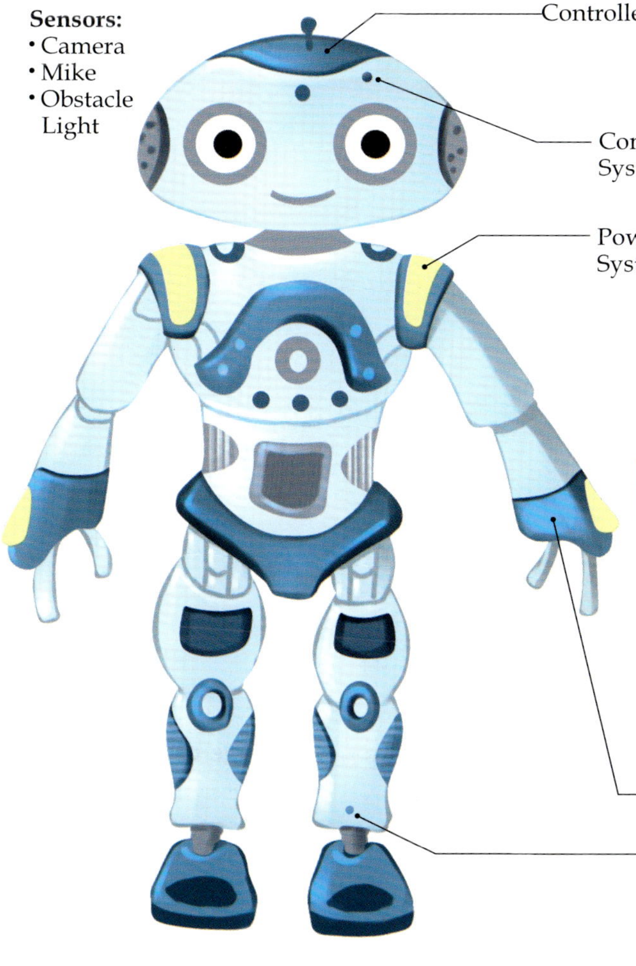

DID YOU KNOW?

Robotics is also a popular hobby. Using their skill and imagination, people have built some interesting robot designs.

2. Programming a Robot

We talk to robots using Robot Software. Robot Software is a set of commands that tell the robot what tasks to perform. Computer languages are used to develop Robot Software.

Learn Robotics Programming

Minibloq is a simple, easy-to-install development tool to learn basic Robotics Programming. It allows you to replicate a physical robot on a computer screen. You can write commands to make the robot move and perform tasks by simply adding code blocks. Minibloq also allows you to connect an actual robot hardware to your computer and run the program on it.

What you'll learn:

- Using the Minibloq editor.
- How to write the basic code for a software robot.
- Understanding the basics of Python code.

POCKET FACT

The top three computer languages used in robotics engineering are C++, Python and Matlab.

Installing Minibloq

Open the Minibloq website by typing http://blog.minibloq.org/p/download.html on your web browser. Click the download link, then run the .exe file to install the Minibloq Software. Take an adult's help to install. Once installed, the Minibloq icon will appear on your desktop.

The Minibloq desktop icon

Minibloq editor

Double click the desktop icon to open the minibloq editor window.

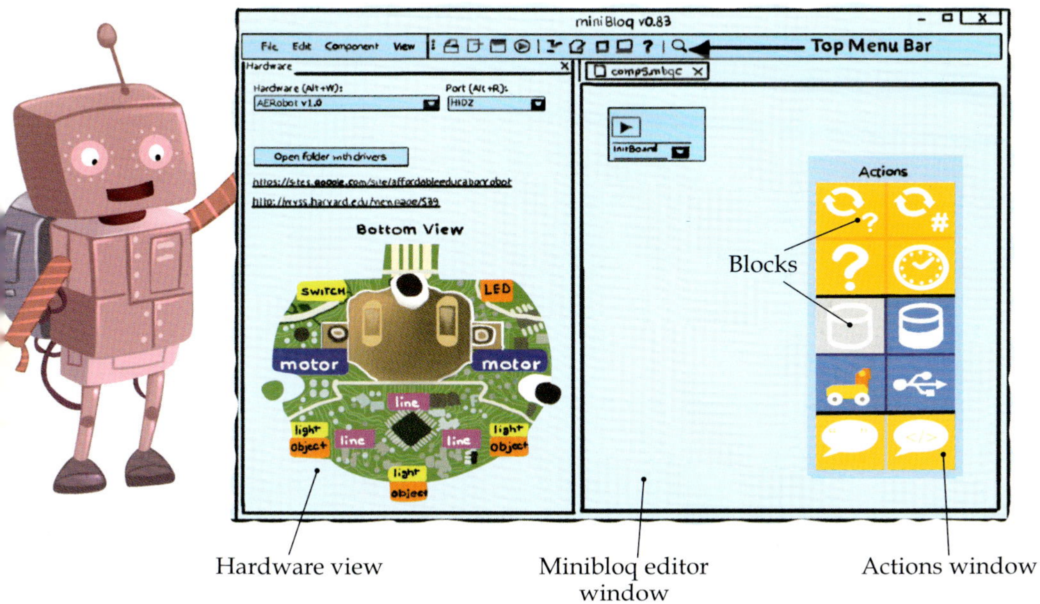

The Minibloq editor is a visual programming tool with code blocks.

DID YOU KNOW?

Minibloq uses drag-and-drop programming that makes coding easy and fun.

3. Working with Minibloq

Let us begin by viewing one of the included examples in Minibloq.

Step 1. Click the 'Hardware' dropdown box and select miniSim. The sprite updates to a robot car.

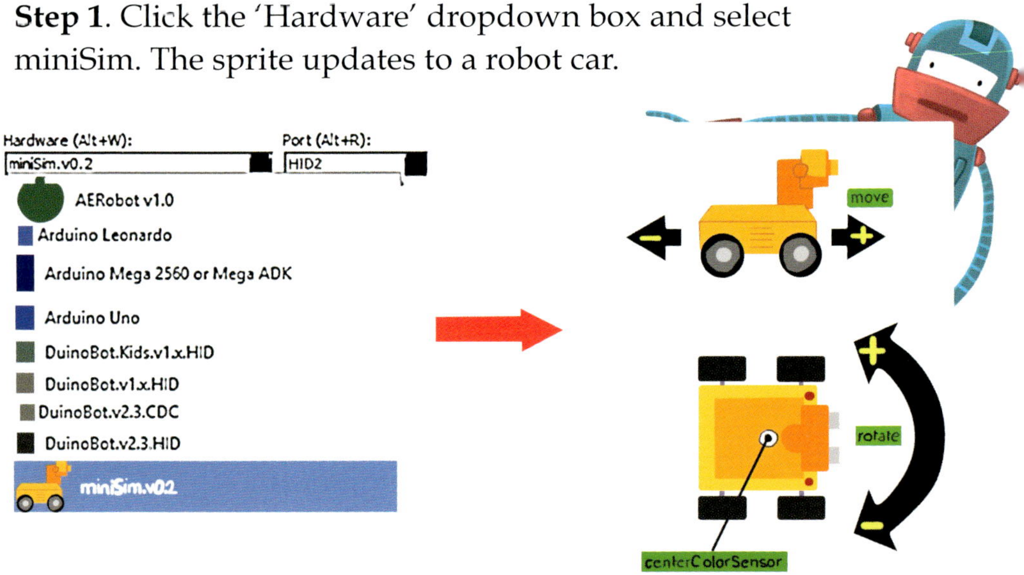

Step 2. Click 'File→Examples' in the top menu to open the list of included examples.

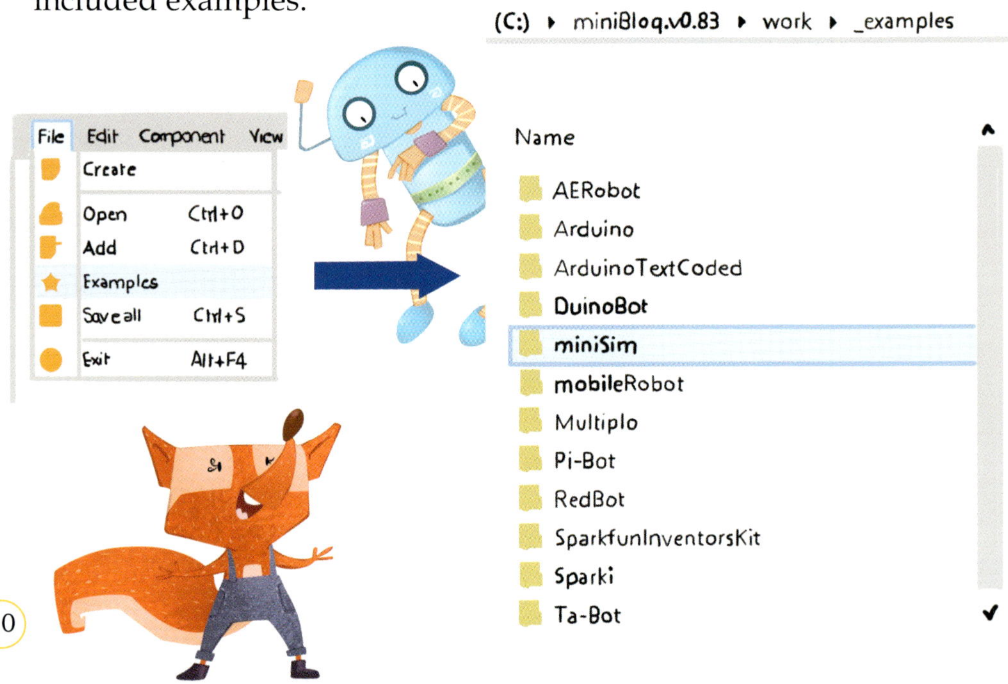

Step 3. Double click to expand the **'miniSim'** folder, then expand the **'10.Square'** folder.

Step 4. Select the **'square.mbqc'** file and click the 'Open' button.

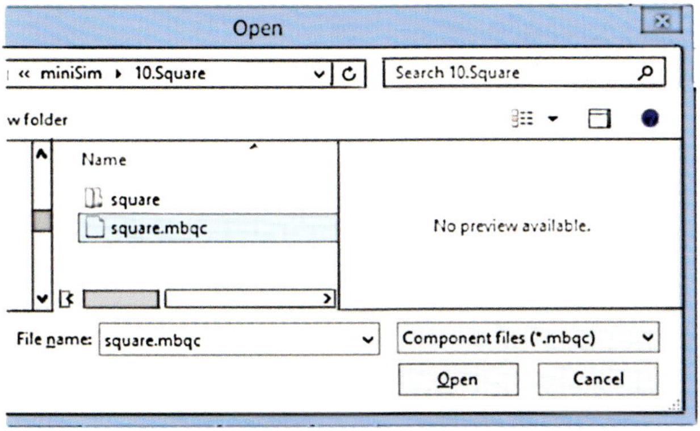

Step 5. The code gets loaded in the editor.

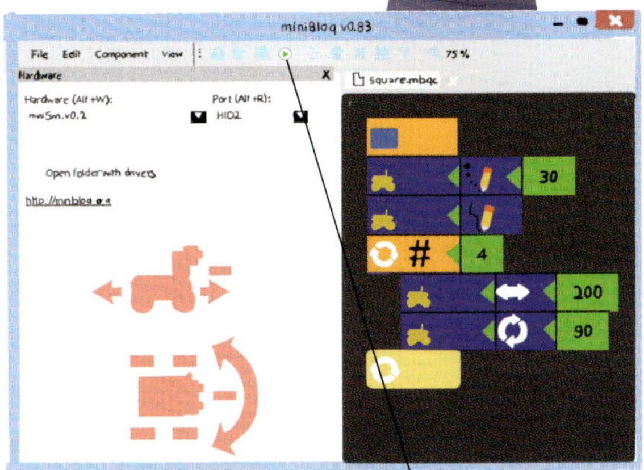

Step 6. Run the code by clicking the green **play** button ▶ in the top menu bar.

Step 7. An output window will popup and show the robot car sprite making a square shape.

What next?

These code blocks actually generate Python code. Open 'View' from the top menu and check the 'Generated code' option.

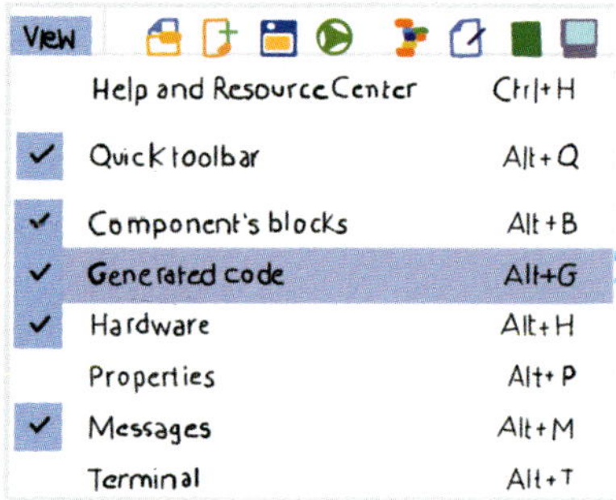

This opens the 'Generated code' view in the Minibloq editor.

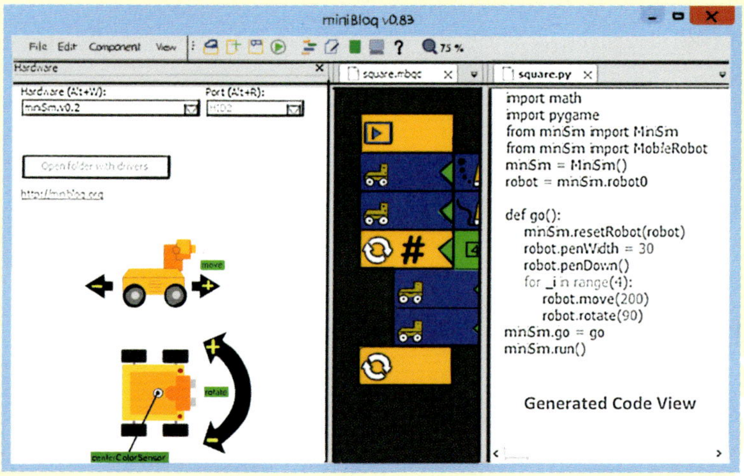

POCKET FACT

Python is a popular and simple computer language used to build desktop software, web applications and mobile apps amongst other things.

What you see in this view is the Python code. These Python commands run the robot. For example, the command -'miniSim. move(200)'-instructs the robot car to move forward by a value of 200.

4. You Too Can Code

Won't it be fun to write your own robotics code? Let's get started.

Goal: Move the miniSim Robot forward and backward.

Step 1. Start a new project

Open the Minibloq editor and click 'File →Create' to start a new project.

Step 2. Select the Hardware

Select miniSim from the Hardware dropdown. The miniSim robot has forward and backward movements. Forward movement is shown as a plus (+) sign, while the backward movement is a minus (-) sign. In the same way, the two directions of rotation are denoted with a '+' or a '-' sign. The robot also has a Colour Sensor.

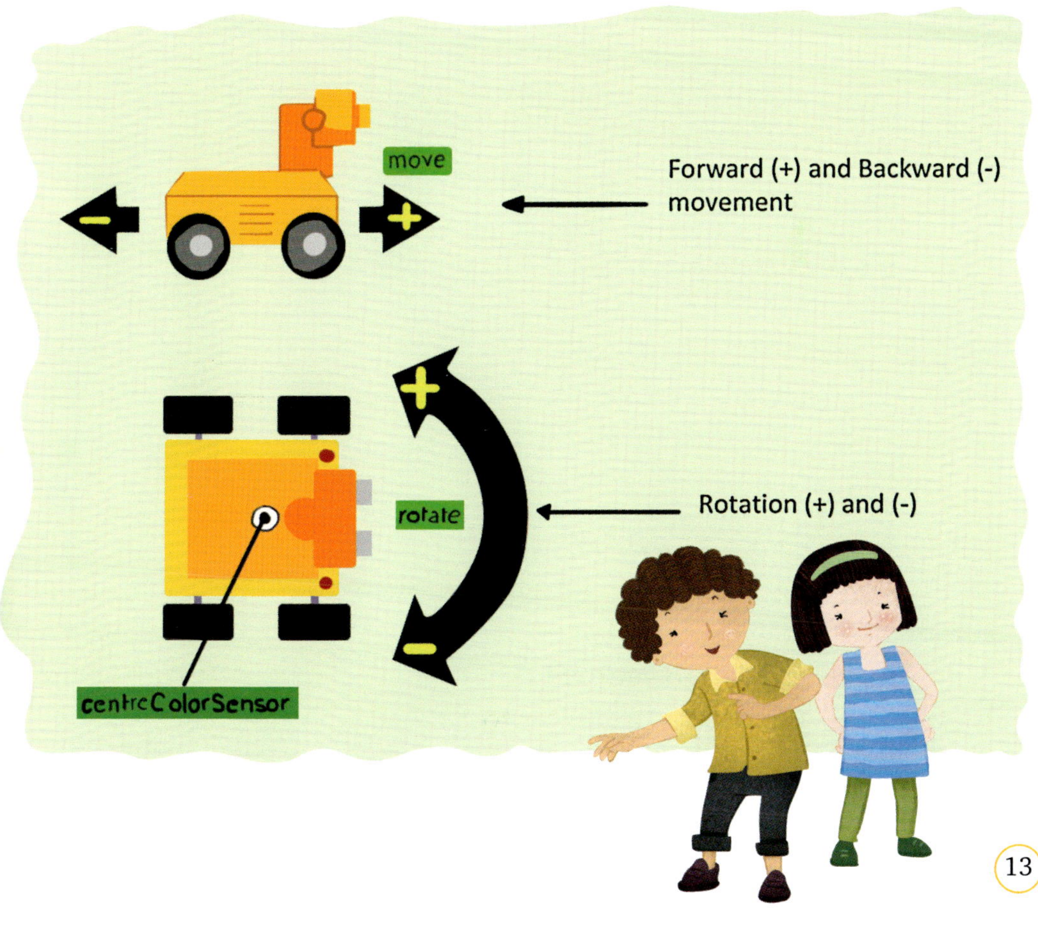

Step 3. Add a forward movement

To add any instruction, click the block from the 'Actions Window'. The block gets added to the grey editor window. Click on the movement block as shown.

Click the red arrow on the movement block. This pops-up further options. The first option represents the forward and backward movement. Select it.

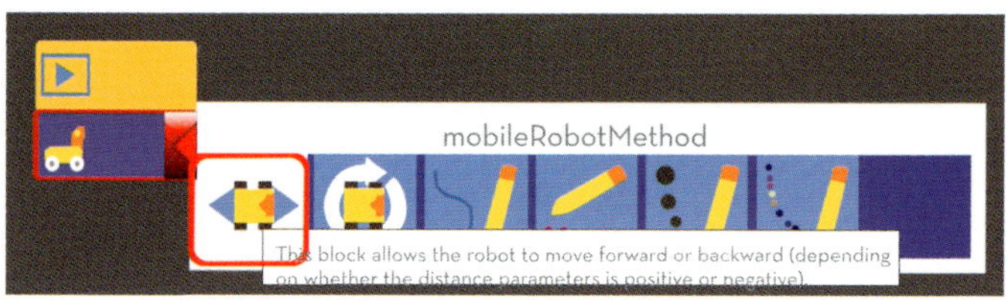

Step 4. Add a movement value

Again click the red arrow and select the '#' block to give a forward movement value.

Change the value to 200 units. If you run the program now, you will see that the robot moves forward by 200 units.

Step 5. Add a reverse movement

Add another movement block as before.

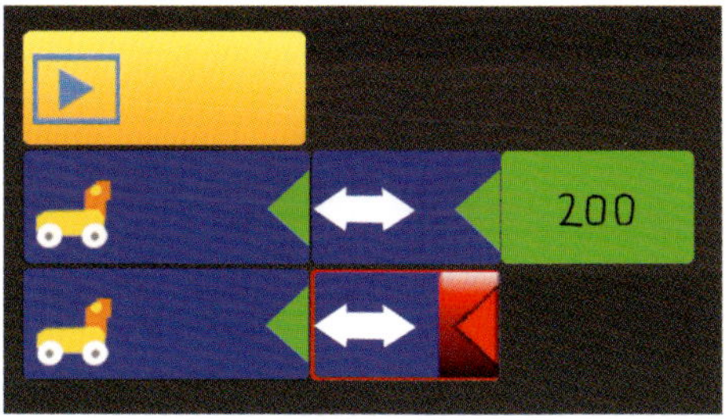

Since we want the robot to move backwards, we need to set a value with a minus sign. Click on the red arrow and select - (×) this time.

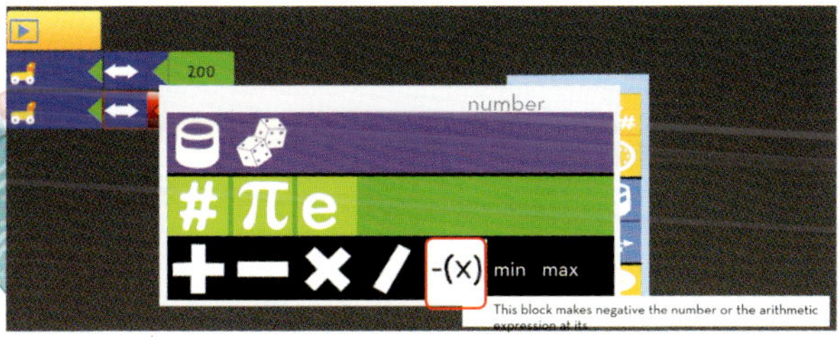

Once again add '#' by clicking on the red arrow on the - (×) block. Change the reverse movement value to 100.

Step 6. Run the program

Click the green play button ▶ and watch the robot car move forward by 200 units, then reverse half the way.

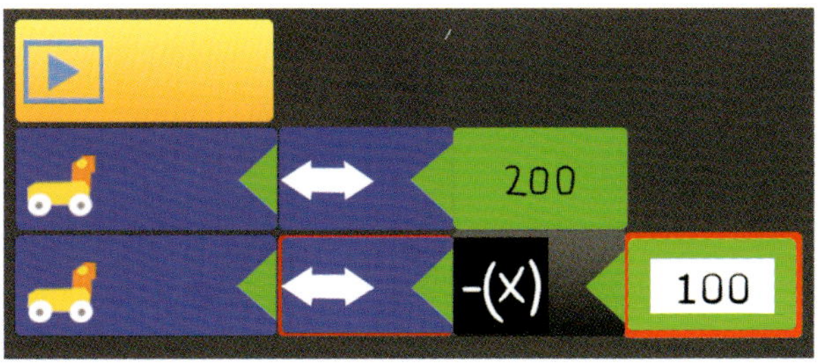

Coding challenge

Change the order of the forward and backward movements and observe the change in the robot's behaviour.

5. Rotating the Robot

Goal: Rotate the miniSim robot.

Step 1. Start a new project and select the miniSim hardware.

Step 2. Add a movement block.

Step 3. Add rotation by selecting the rotation block.

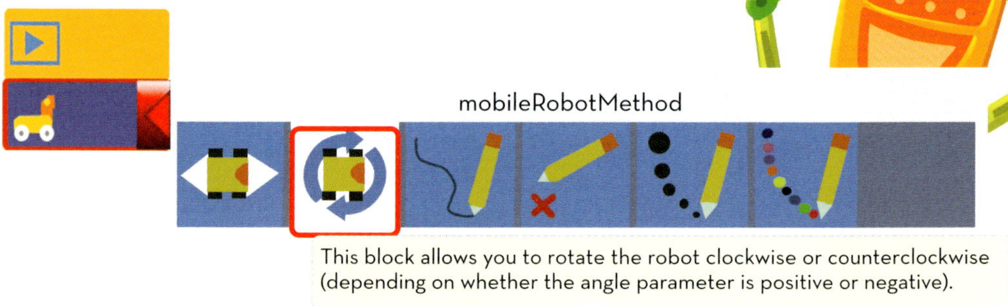

Step 4. Add a value for the rotation by clicking on the red arrow and selecting '#'. Change the rotation value to 90.

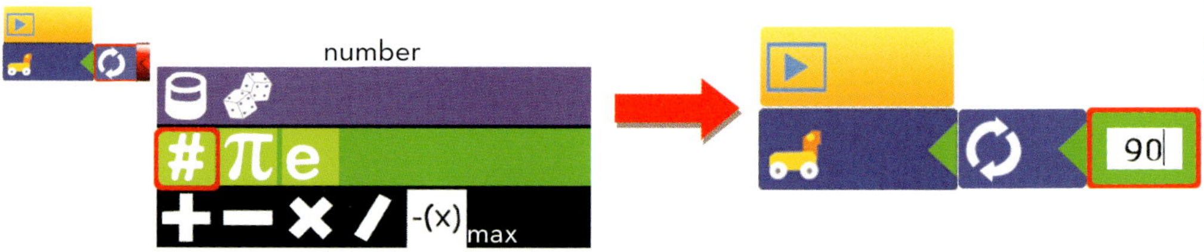

Step 5. If you run this program, the robot will turn left by 90 degrees.

Step 6. To make the robot turn right add a -(x) instruction before the # value:

Step 7. Run this program to see the robot turn right by 90 degrees.

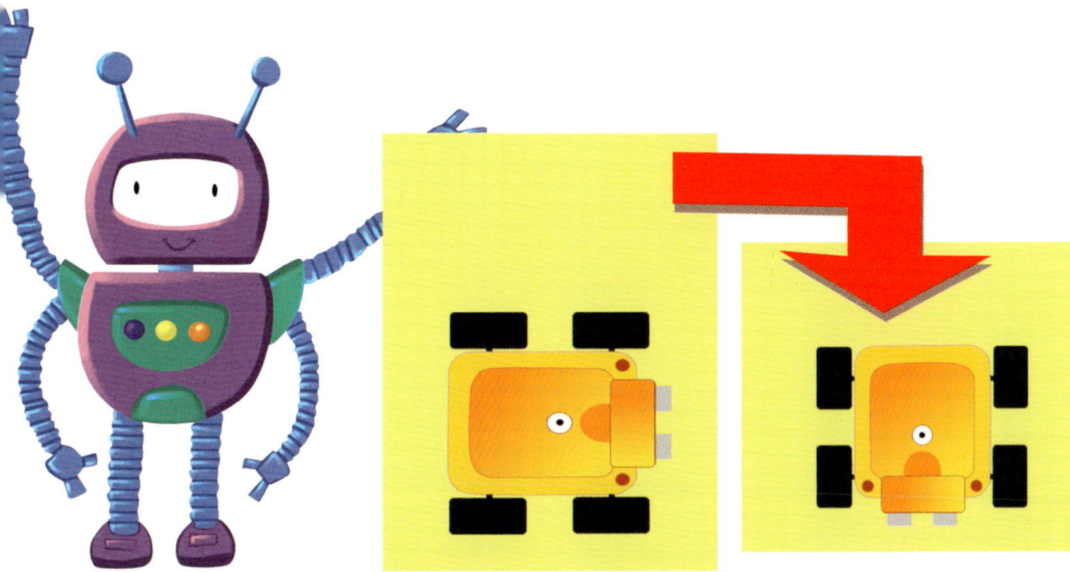

Coding Challenge

Make the robot move along a square path. Hint: Repeat the forward movement and left rotation instructions four times.

6. A Drawing Robot

In the example, we saw the robot draw a square. In the same way we can make it draw other shapes too.

Goal: Make the robot draw a shape.

Step 1. Start a new project and select the miniSim hardware.

Step 2. Add a movement block as before.

Step 3. We want the robot to draw, so we have to instruct it to put its 'pencil down' first. Select the third option in the list.

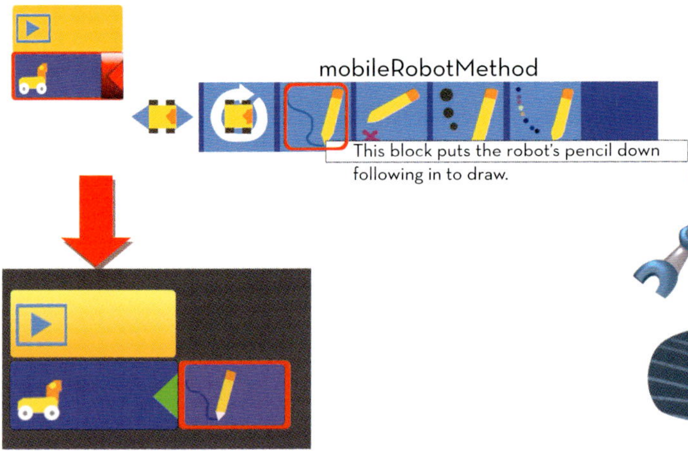

Step 4. Next we want it to move and draw a straight line of 100 units.

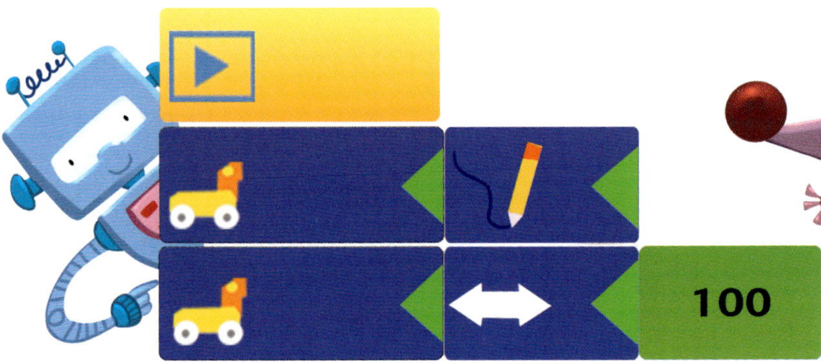

Run the code now to see the robot draw a straight line.

Step 5. Add further code to draw a square.

Coding Challenge

Draw a rectangle. Hint: A rectangle is similar to a square, but with the opposite sides having equal length.

7. Tips and Tricks

Save your code

Press 'Ctrl+S' buttons on your keyboard or click on 'File → Save All' in the top menu to save your program. Give a suitable name to your program file when asked for and press the 'Save' button. To open a saved program, use the 'File→Open' menu option.

Removing a block

To remove a block from your instruction set, right-click the block with your mouse and select 'delete'.

Alternatively, you can also select the block to remove, then click on 'Edit→Cut' from the top menu bar.

Inserting a block

Sometimes we want to insert a new block between two blocks. To do this, first select the block below which you wish to insert a new block. Then add a new block as usual by clicking in the 'Actions Window'.

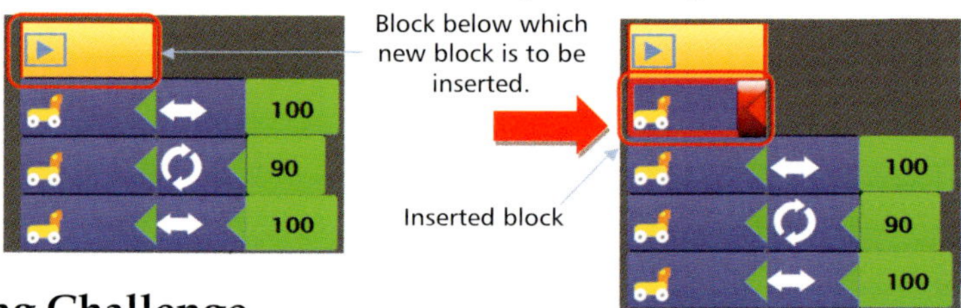

Coding Challenge

Cut an existing block from your code and paste it at another position. Hint-Use the 'Edit→Cut' and 'Edit→Paste' menu items from the top menu.

Changing the pencil's colour

To draw a red line, change the pencil's colour first.

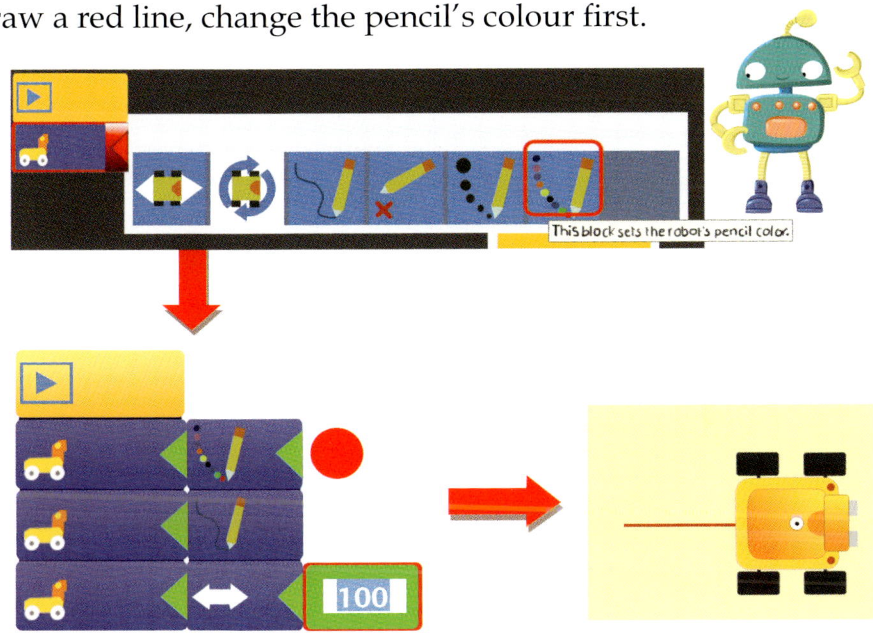

Changing the pencil's width

To draw a thicker line, change the pencil's width first.

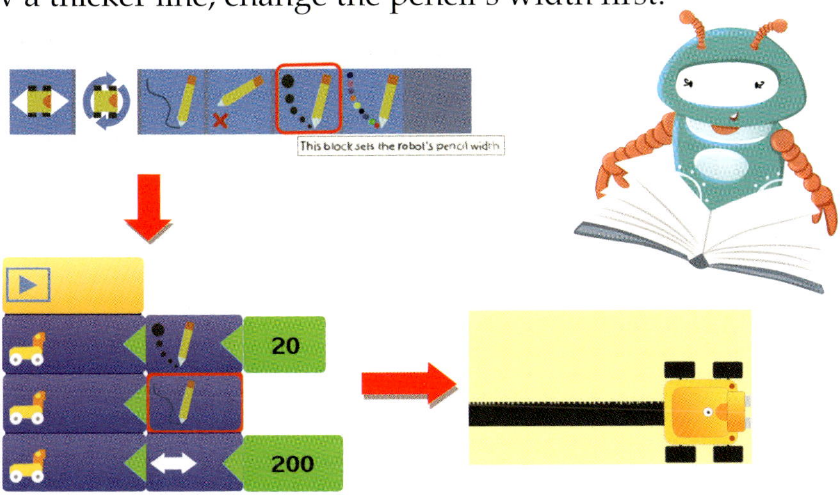

Coding Challenge

Draw a red square of thickness 20. Hint- You need to set the pencil colour and thickness only once in your program.

8. Loops

To make a square, you had to write the instructions - ' draw a straight line, then turn by 90 degrees' - four times in your program. In other words, you told the robot to:

1) Walk 100 units. Turn 90 degrees.

2) Walk 100 units. Turn 90 degrees.

3) Walk 100 units. Turn 90 degrees.

4) Walk 100 units. Turn 90 degrees.

Wouldn't it be better if we could just say:
Repeat these steps 4 times:

- Walk 100 units. Turn 90 degrees.

'Loops' allow us to do just that.

Loops in the Action Window

There are two types of Loops in Minibloq coding:

1. **Repeat loop** - This repeats a set of instructions for a given 'number' of times. For instance, when making a square, we want the robot to repeat the steps '4' times.

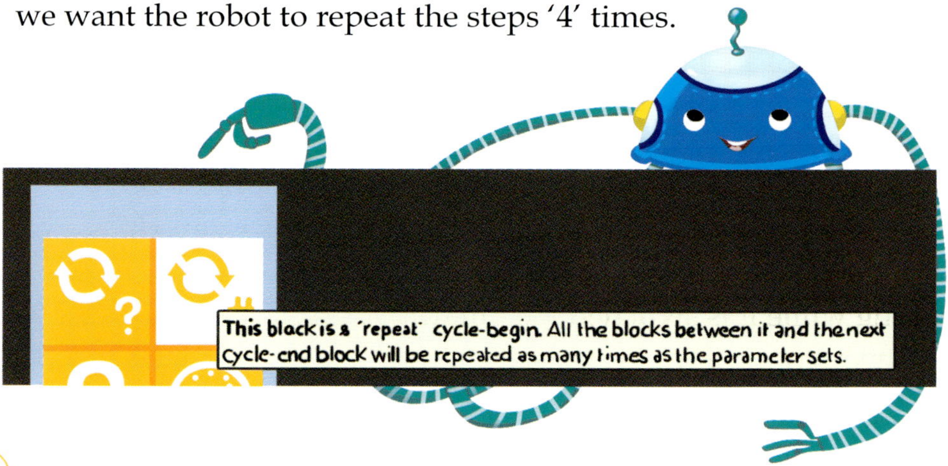

2. **While loop** - This loop repeats a set of instructions while a condition is true.

To understand this type of loop, pretend you have a bag of chips. You will keep eating chips as long as there is something in the bag. The fan is another while-loop in real-life. It keeps running while it is switched 'on'. In fact, if the fan is never switched off, it will run forever.

Repeated loop in action

Let's modify our code to make a square using loops.

Step 1. Create a new project and select the pencil settings.

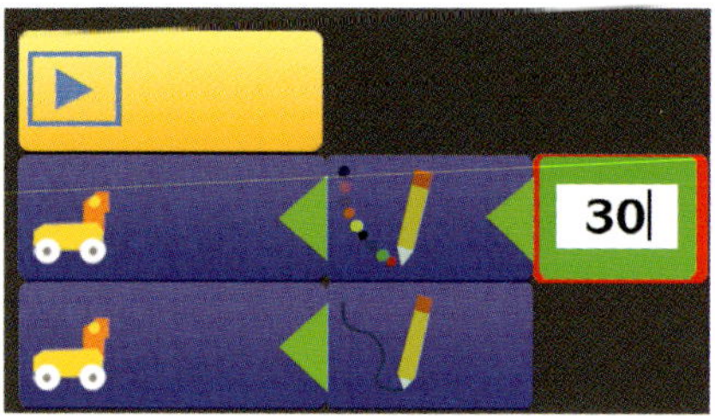

Step 2. Add the repeat loop and change the value to '4'.

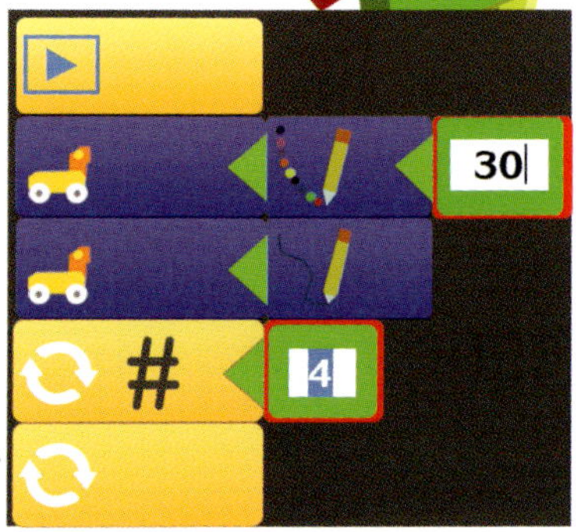

Step 3. Now add the steps to draw a straight line and then turn 90 degrees.

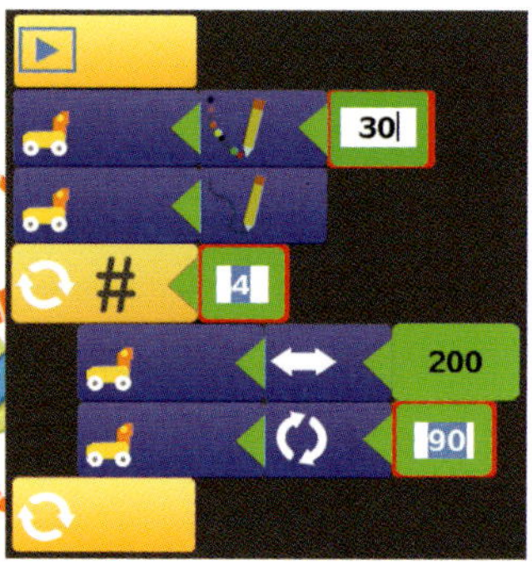

Step 4. Run this code. The robot repeats the instructions four times - draw a straight line, then turn 90 degrees. The result is a square shape.

While-loop

What will happen if you replace the repeat-loop in the program with a while-loop? Let's see.

Step 1. Create a new project and select the pencil settings.

Step 2. Add a while-loop. Then click on the red arrow and select the first condition block. This 'condition' block always returns 'true'. In other words, we are setting a 'forever' loop.

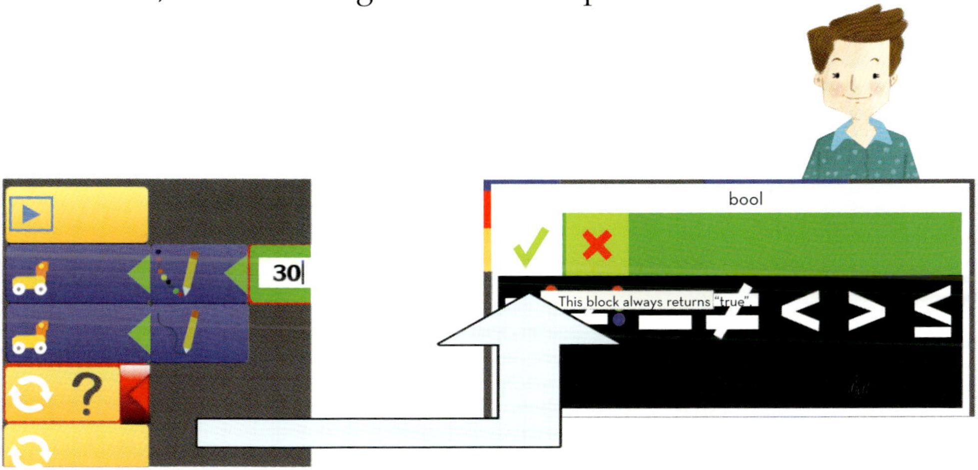

Step 3. Now add the blocks for drawing the square.

Step 4. What happens when you run this program? The robot keeps drawing a square over and over again.

9. Decoding Python

Let us take a look at the Python code too. The python code generated for the repeat-loop was this-

```
robot.penWidth = 30
robot.penDown()
for _i in range(4):
robot.move(100)
robot.rotate(90)
```

Here is what each Python code tells the robot to do:

robot.penwidth = 30 →	Sets the width of the pen for the robot.
robot.pendown() →	Puts the robot's pen down in order to start drawing.
for_i in range(4): →	This is the start of the 'repeat loop'. This loop runs '4' times.
robot.move(100) →	Instructs the robot to move forward by 100 units.
robot.rotate(90) →	Instructs the robot to turn left by 90 degrees.

What you learnt

You learnt how to generate Minibloq code for the miniSim robot. View different examples included with Minibloq and write some more codes on your own.

10. Artificial Intelligence

We programmed a robot to walk, turn and draw shapes. But did the computer program make the robot 'intelligent'?

Intelligence is using your knowledge and experience to take decisions. If you've once touched a hot stove, you will not touch it again because you know that it burns. So, while the robot followed your program to draw a square, it did not use that experience to draw a rectangle. Unlike you, the robot does not have intelligence.

What is AI?

'Artificial Intelligence (AI)' is simply a machine's ability to think and learn like a human. Siri and Alexa are two voice-controlled bots that we can talk to as if talking to a person. They use AI to successfully understand human speech.

Chess and Go are complex gaming systems based on AI. They understand their opponents' moves and develop their strategy as the game progresses.

While AI enables machines to solve problems, scientists are yet to create a machine that is creative and has feelings like us.

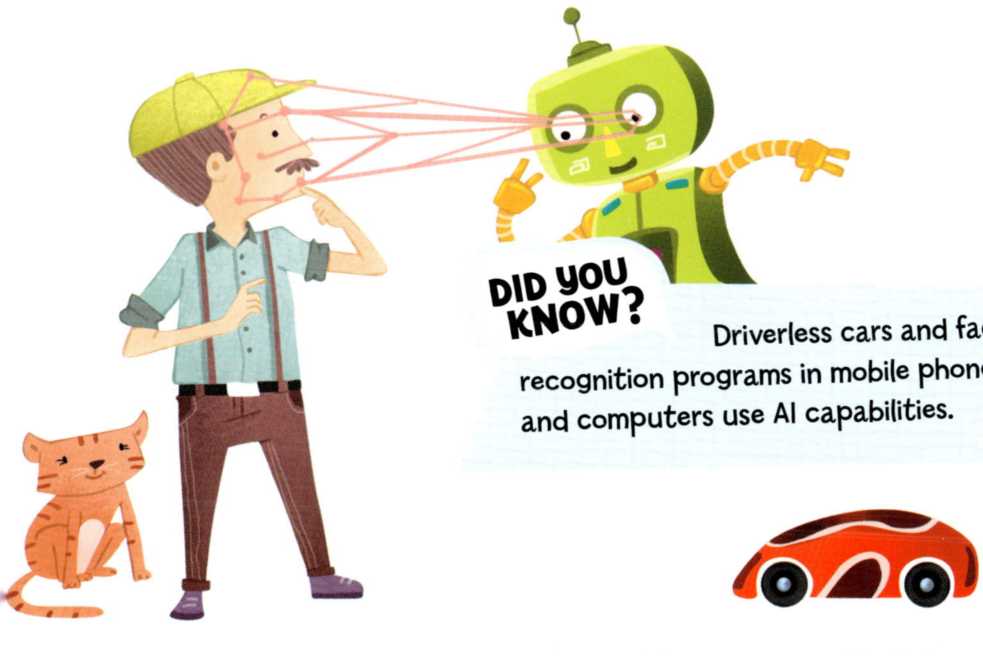

DID YOU KNOW?

Driverless cars and face recognition programs in mobile phones and computers use AI capabilities.

Let's Get Active

Robot Word Search

ARTIFICIAL	COMPUTER	FUTURE	HUMANOID
INTELLIGENCE	MACHINE	PROGRAM	RECOGNITION
SENSORS	TECHNOLOGY		

I	T	E	C	H	N	O	L	O	G	Y	T	V
N	S	E	N	S	O	R	S	F	K	C	O	K
T	V	Y	W	K	E	P	G	U	R	B	G	X
E	P	R	O	G	R	A	M	T	B	F	N	C
L	M	Z	Z	F	O	X	T	U	P	O	X	O
L	A	A	K	D	A	N	D	R	O	I	D	M
I	C	C	W	A	A	O	L	E	T	U	T	P
G	H	U	M	A	N	O	I	D	D	N	T	U
E	I	A	X	M	T	X	F	D	O	V	E	T
N	N	A	R	T	I	F	I	C	I	A	L	E
C	E	C	H	E	R	K	I	L	C	A	R	R
E	V	V	P	S	F	X	Q	V	E	R	V	C
H	N	R	E	C	O	G	N	I	T	I	O	N

Robotics Quiz

Choose the correct answer:

1. What is Robotics?
   (a) Playing with tools.
   (b) Studying Stars.
   (c) Learning about creating robots or machines that can do work.
2. How are robots created?
   (a) They grow on trees.
   (b) They're built by robotics engineers and scientists.
   (c) Anyone can build them using blocks.
3. A robot that resembles a human is called a
   (a) Asimo
   (b) Curiosity
   (c) Humanoid
4. Which of these a robot cannot do in today's world?
   (a) Author a book
   (b) Mow the lawn
   (c) Build other robots
5. We can talk to robots using
   (a) Robot Software
   (b) Speakers
   (c) Microphone

What will the robot do?

What will this Minibloq code make the miniSim robot do?

Choose the correct option:

1. Draw a line
2. Draw a green square
3. Draw a green circle
4. Draw a blue rectangle

Let's Save the World

Match the type of pollution to the solution for the problem.

Air Pollution	Soundproofing
Water Pollution	Adding bacteria
Soil Pollution	Renewable energy
Noise Pollution	Mr. Trash Wheel

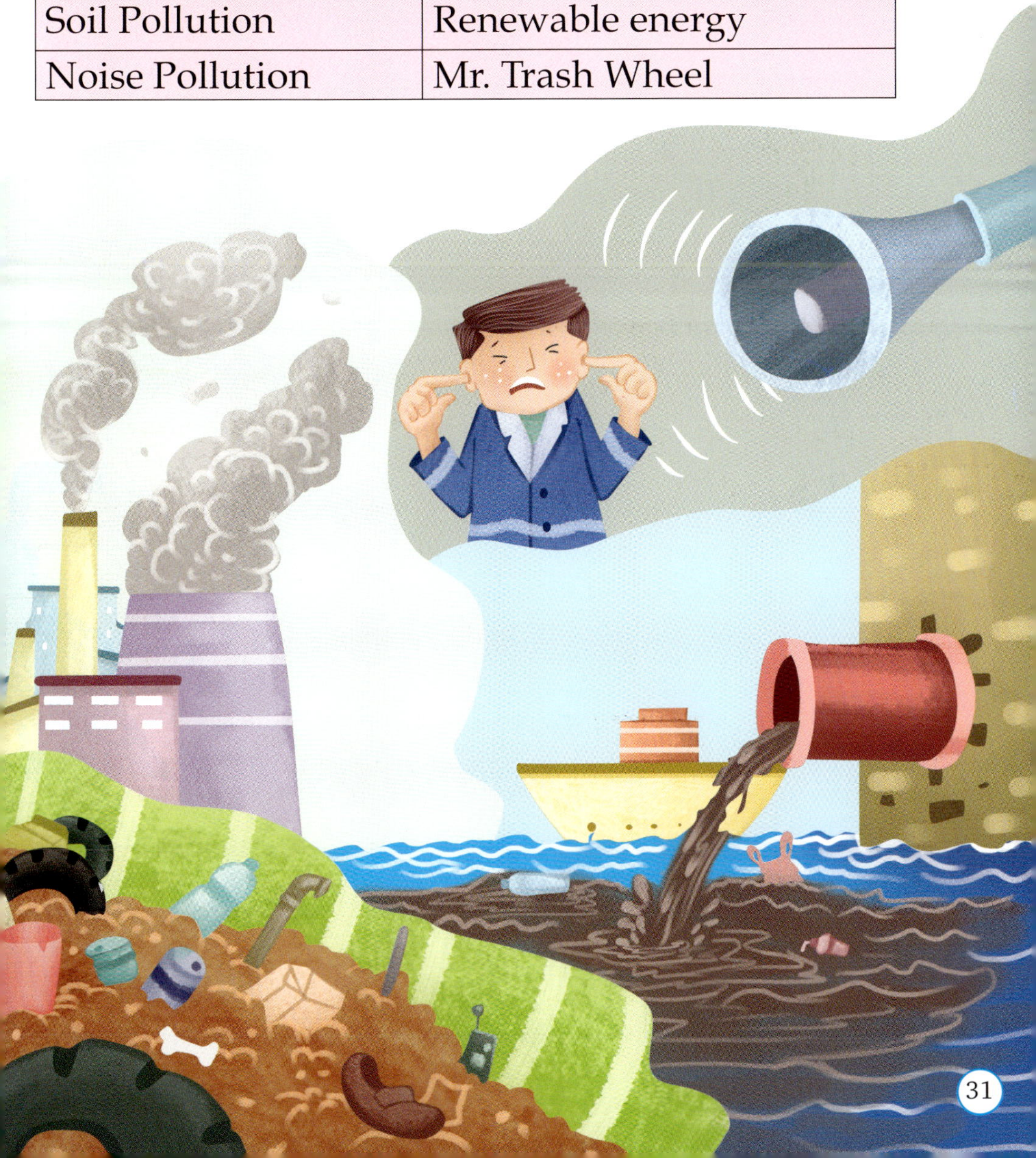

GLOSSARY

Activist	a person who campaigns to bring about political or social change.
Anxious	worried, tensed
Belch	to burp
Communicate	share or exchange information
Impact	affect
Litter	garbage
Nuisance	thing causing inconvenience
Organism	a living thing
Pollutant	a substance that pollutes something
Preserve	maintain or keep alive
Reduce	lessen
Submarine	a warship that can travel underwater
Toxic	poisonous

ANSWERS

Page 28. boat, umbrella, beach chair, book, ball, mat, glasses, hat, carry bag, signboard

Page 29. 1. Air 2. Water 3. Air and Water 4. Soil 5. Air 6. Noise

Page 30.
1. Treatment Centre
2. Screens
3. Primary Settlement Tanks
4. Aeration Chamber
5. Walls and Roofs
6. River

Page 31. Air Pollution-Renewable energy
Water Pollution-Mr. Trash Wheel
Soil Pollution-Adding bacteria
Noise Pollution-Soundproofing